LINDSAY MANN

Beyond Love

A COLLECTION OF CHANNELED MESSAGES FROM PASSED-ON LOVED ONES

HEY CLARITY
HARTSDALE, NY

Lindsay Mann
Hey Clarity

www.heyclarity.com

Beyond Love: A Collection of Channeled Messages from Passed-On Loved Ones / Lindsay Mann —1st ed.

Paperback ISBN 979-8-9863954-0-1
Hardcover ISBN 979-8-9863954-1-8

Dedicated to my Loved Ones in Spirit
… and beyond.

PROLOGUE

The timing of the completion of this book is bittersweet. I set off to inspire and warm the hearts of those grieving the loss of Loved Ones, and in the process, I am confronted with losing a dear Loved One of my own. No matter how many words of comfort are offered and received, the pain still aches. The grief and heartbreak come in waves, and nothing can take that away except, maybe, time.

Our Soul connections between all those we cherish run deep. We find each other throughout lifetimes in different faces and forms. We might recognize each other upon our reunions and rejoice, but saying goodbye always hurts.

If you are mourning the loss of a Loved One, however recent or long ago, my heart goes out to you as a fellow human being. Cry until you can laugh, celebrate, and honor your time shared together. But, please know that whoever you are grieving loves you and misses you too. And they want you to know that they'll be with you every step of the way.

INVITATION

Stillness. Be still. It will come to you. Sit up straight or lie down. Relax into the space you're in. Be there without planning on doing anything. You're not doing; you're being. Just be and breathe.

"I am open to receiving" is a helpful intention to set in your mind or say aloud. Do nothing else. Receptivity is your position. In receiving, you are relaxed and welcoming. Energetically, you are drawing things towards yourself. Let go of all expectations. Do not try to force anything to happen.

Slowly become aware of the subtle things around you—the sounds, smells, sensations. What's yours, and what's coming from somewhere else? Note the distinction. Get to know your sounds and your body's sensations. They are always giving you information. Once you become familiar with the totality of you, it'll be easier to recognize what isn't coming from you. Take the time to get to know yourself inside and out.

Spirit has ways of gripping our attention through our bodies. The more important the message, the more powerful the experience will be to get our attention. You'll know because it will be something just out of the ordinary or repetitive. Don't ignore it or shut it down. Instead, listen, be patient, and spend time with it to receive the information that's being given to you.

You'll start to notice that certain sensations are felt at certain times. For example, often, when I'm in conversation with people, I might feel a chill brush up my left calf as a confirmation of, "Yes! Keep talking; what you're saying is resonating." Other times, I might feel a building of heat or hear an audible ringing in my ears. That means I'm being signaled to stop, be still, pay attention to my surroundings, and listen for something important. I've recognized these sensations and what I become aware of after feeling them over years of paying attention to them.

These are "tells." A multitude of combinations of consistent tells will ping you in your daily life at certain moments. I initially thought this was my intuition or Higher Self, but have since learned that they are cues from my Passed-On Loved Ones.

One even alerts me through a tickle on my top front tooth, like a "sweet tooth," a reference relevant to our bond. When I feel this sensation, I know to ask this specific Passed-On Loved One, "Hey, is there something I need to know here?" To which they reply with a message for me about my direct experience.

Whether you find it easy to connect or not, this book documents what Passed-On Loved Ones have shared with me about this exact time in our living history. It's an honor to share their words with you, and I hope they shed light on your life and inspire you as much as they have for me.

I invite you to read this book with the playful divination practice of Stichomancy, randomly selecting passages and pages to get the messages you need at this time.

INTRODUCTION

What if, when we die, we go everywhere?

What if we could see everything from the widest lens and the highest perspective?

What if the gunk and guts of being human could simplify into an essence of an ethereal core?

What if the imprint of our unique energetic expression continues to exist without our bodies?

And what if that energetic expression could hold a presence and communicate through subtleties?

The messages in this book were received from unique energetic expressions that hold a presence in my life and communicate through subtleties. Some of them are with me all the time—those are my personal Guides/Angels/Passed-On Loved Ones—and others connect with me in passing as I invite them.

My intention with their messages is to normalize a profound source of support that we are often taught to shut down, fear, or not believe in, which otherwise would provide immeasurable love, guidance, and wisdom.

If any words in this book give you goosebumps, chills, or other sensory reactions while reading them, someone may be saying a very loving, "Hello," to you from the other side. The first person who comes to mind is most likely who it is. So say, "Hello," back. They'll be thrilled to reconnect.

We choose when to reincarnate. The connection won't be possible if a Passed-On Loved One is off into their next chapter in a new form. You might meet them again, in their new life, in the future. We do this a lot. But many choose to stick around us until they know we're going to be ok.

No matter your beliefs or abilities to connect, you are supported by Passed-On Loved Ones. In my experience, life is monumentally more fascinating knowing I have them by my side, guiding me through it all. I hope this loving exploration opens your eyes to the vast existence of our consciousness beyond living life and our most beloved connections, unseen yet known.

Beginnings

BEGINNINGS

When I first became aware of my connection with Spirit, I reunited with a particular Passed-On Loved One over a couple of weeks. It began with a guided Shamanic journey led by my Shamanic healer. I reconnected with this Loved One while journeying through the Underworld.

As I lay there with my eyes closed, following my healer's guidance, exploring, and receiving symbolic references, I felt someone join me. I saw cover art visuals from a record that specifically reminded me of this person, and their name kept repeating in my head. This Loved One will be referred to as "S" throughout the book.

I was consumed and distracted by S's presence, and at the end of my session, I asked my healer, "Are you getting anything around the name, S? They took over my journey." My healer replied, "Yes! S is saying, 'Hey! I think you can help me!'"

Immediately after the session ended, I felt a series of clear sensations. First, my ears warmed up from the inside. Then I felt a slight breeze against my right ear as if a person was sitting next to me blowing into it. It was playful and teasing in a way that made me swat at my ear. It was S.

Words started coming to me quickly, almost audibly: "My mom is sad. Can you help me?" I replied aloud automatically with a list of ways S could connect with their mother to comfort her and let her know they were around. I somehow knew what to say, and it totally surprised me—not to mention my nonchalance speaking out loud to an empty room.

The rest of my day was hijacked by S's presence. I felt them sitting next to me in the passenger seat of my car wherever I drove. We had conversations of sorts, as if I was hanging out with any other friend. It blew my mind, and I thought I was going crazy.

The weeks that followed felt fated. I had two more healing sessions with two completely different intuitive practitioners. S came through to talk to me in each session, taking advantage of the clear communication channels to explain the importance of our reunion. Through them, S told me that I could connect with plants, animals, and Spirit greater than I had ever realized, that this was my work in the world, and that S would teach me mediumship as a gift to strengthen those abilities.

It was a massive victory in S's eyes, as they had been trying to connect with me for years. I felt their triumph; I felt their honor; and I felt an adoration that moved me.

We practiced communicating through automatic writing in journals at first. I jotted down Q & A conversations between us and S's poetry to distinguish between my thoughts and S's words. Eventually, we moved to type on the computer keyboard for faster communication.

One day, S directed me to old boxes in my childhood home where I initially thought we were digging for pictures and memories of when I knew them. Cleverly, S led me to a box of my artwork from high school.

Inside were drawings, paintings, and sketches of people. People I didn't know and people whose faces looked sad, even tormented. I remembered creating those artworks alone in my bedroom during emotional times of catharsis, expressing myself through them, or so I thought.

S told me that I had been channeling Souls from the other side through my artwork. And though I didn't realize it, my connection to Spirit had been lifelong. Therefore, I couldn't determine something as innate to be anything out of the ordinary. I had the relationship, felt it around me, but never knew what it was or that I could do anything with it.

I started to remember all the times I felt recently deceased Loved Ones still around after their death. And I began to understand why, throughout my life, I just knew things and could see through things that others couldn't fathom.

Since having my first connection with S, I've connected with hundreds of Spirits. Their presence to me is as unique and prominent in energy as living people. When they know I'm listening for them, they share their perspectives about the world, my environment, my choices, and the people I encounter in my life. They protect, comfort, and inform me, and they open my world up to its limitlessness.

In our time together, my Passed-On Loved Ones have shown me devotion so absolute and unconditional that it can't be expressed through words but rather is felt in the quiet between them. They have reminded me to my core that our consciousness is beyond measure, and so is our love.

Akashic Records
On Spirit

AKASHIC RECORDS
ON SPIRIT

The Akashic Records provide wisdom from the highest perspective on you and everyone connected to you. They inform our consciousness of ultimate truths that speak directly to our Soul.

I channel guidance from the Akashic Records as my work, connecting people to the Soul's perspective on life experiences and the world. I appreciate the Records' way of grounding any concept into knowledge that we can all digest and understand.

My favorite definition of the Akashic Records comes from Hungarian philosopher of Science, Ervin László: "The electromagnetic imprint of everything that's ever happened in the Universe." He explains that the Universe conserves information in an information field that is the Akashic realm.

To offer clarification and the most definitive examples of Spirit /Passed-On Loved Ones/Angels/Ghosts/etc., I opened the Akashic Records on Spirit for their interpretation of the subject.

On the following pages, you'll find the channeled reading I conducted with the Akashic Records on Spirit.

What does it mean to be in Spirit?

No longer here

in Earth realm

and form.

What's the difference between Spirit/
Passed-On Loved Ones/Angels/
Ghosts/etc.?

Same thing.

Different types of relationships to you.

Closer

or farther away

in relation to you

in your current life.

What does it feel like
to be in Spirit form?

F r e e e e e —

Very loose,

open, wispy, fluid,

movement

speedy and s l o w.

Slippery, smokey, ethereal,

playful, joyful,

simplified form.

Easy. Breezy. See-through.

Us and all.

Transparent, clear,

ultimate clarity.

How long can we be in Spirit form?

Seamless.

No seams. No end. No barriers.

Up to you, ultimately,
when to go into a new form.

Dive in again.

Up to you, when ready.

Surely ready.

Raring to go!

Jump in. Soul jumps back in.

How far can Spirit travel?

Limitless.

Any time.

Any place.

To anyone.

Everywhere.

Ever in existence.

How does Spirit want to be described?

Ultimate love and freedom.

It can be felt and experienced
in the living human form too.

Very liberating and comforting to be
encapsulated in a body while feeling the
ultimate love and freedom of your Spirit.

It's a big issue in the world,
not understanding how meaningful life is.

Physical form packs a punch energetically.
Spirit isn't in form; it's not materialized.

What's the relationship between the living and Spirit today?

You have been dialing in more recently and have become more open and honest about understanding the living human spirit.
Your expansive form, energetically. How big you are.
Take up more space in living.
Take up space in this world.

Bodies form, and energies form. Together.
As one. Yours and Spirit's.   Intertwined.
United. Earthly and Heavenly reunited.
You belong together as one working mechanism interwoven across the lands.   Use it.
Use them wisely. Purposefully, intentionally.
On purpose. For purpose.

Work to make this connection regularly.
A massive shift in collective consciousness with it, for the best. For the world.   Open up.
Ask for help. Always. Never closed.
24/7 Worldwide connection.

What do we need to understand about dark or "evil" Spirits?

A precarious entity with a trapped mind on Earth.
Of lower vibrational Earthly consciousness—
deep regret, fear, shame, guilt, sadness, or anger.
The mind has not lifted or let go of Earthly life.
Being encapsulated in the Earthly realm is
comforting. However, long-term,
intense energy pulls down.

If a living person is unaware, surrendered,
or compromised, the body can fill up with entities
stubborn to continue living on Earth.
Powerful energy but also simply energy.
Not forever. Temporary energetic matches.
Vibrational matches.
Once the living person lifts energy,
the lower energy of the entity
cannot continue living in it.

Spirits + alcohol/drugs + feeling low
= takedown for a ride. Takeover. The conflicts
that arise during takeovers are not necessarily
between the living.
The "control" issues are between the
taken over and an entity but
cannot be acknowledged as such.
Know this! Takeovers are a reality but only
happen when a living human vessel
is "left unattended." The results may become
dangerous, thrilling, or violent.
The entities are acting out to feel alive.

However, the general experience of Spirit is like
feeling the sun on your face, forehead, eyes,
throat, heart. The upper body Chakras connect
with Spirit while the lower Chakras are of
the Earthly realm. The balance of two worlds
flowing and activated. Between two worlds.

What are the most important messages we need to know about Spirit?

Spirit is a constant flood of energies from Earth into "Space." Movement. Uniquely, individual. The power of movement gathered to rise. Spirit automatically upgrades the energy of the Soul once in Spirit form. It moves everywhere, intentionally, purposefully, without question. Clear strings of consciousness. Precise, concise energies. Ultimate clarity. Clear eyes, clearest skies. Transparent. Not visible forms. Invisible, but felt. It's feeling, energy. A sensed individual. Felt through the senses, insights— inner knowledge and wisdom givers and receivers.

Spirit covers, protects, secures, directs, redirects, moves obstacles, gives ideas, and is ever-present in your life. Indestructible in form. Non-reactive. Proactive. Spirit is always moving energetically up and forward, raising consciousnesses. Once tapped into the energy, you are lifted and uplifted.

Messages From Passed-On Loved Ones

MARIANNE

You'll see in time the monumental shifts in the world for the good of all. We believe in you from Heaven not to destroy what you hold Sacred; all that you love, that loves you, in life. We believe your hearts are bigger than any underlying insecurities or fears. Atrocity stems from fear—love blooms in the aftermath. Love prevails. Hate surrenders when melted in loss and heartbreak. Allow the heartbreak. Beneath the hate, rage, and fear, is sadness and longing, protected. Longing for love and nurturing that may not be visible at times.

Believe in us to be there for you, to love you, to keep you safe, and to guide you along. Listen for us in dark times. We are calling to you, but you must stop and listen. You are hearing us. Don't discount your instincts. Trust your body. The feelings of yes, no, stop, or go. Listen for us. Ask us for help when you are in need. We'll pull through for you. Anywhere, anytime. It's the greatest blessing of dying to be everywhere beside you for as long as we do. When we leave here to go back there or elsewhere, we pass the torch to your next helpers. You are always supported.

Still Beats

Nestled in the Earth
Here and now
Above it all
Below the falls
Right as rain
Cleansing our ashes
Dust to dust
Boy to man
Man to sand
Waves of the ocean
Coast in my eyes
Depths of seas
Heights of skies
Here lies me
In front of you
My heart
Still beats
Inside of you
I forgot to remember
Why I became
You see me with you
You still say my name
I forgot to remember
We live on forever

—S

GERTRUDE

Our brains have a way of forgetting who we are, our limitless-ness—captured in false narratives around being and existing. The eternal frightens us somehow when we're living, perhaps because there's so much pain and suffering. How could we possibly do this forever? But we do.

The fear is not of the end. The fear is of eternal existence. On and on and on. Death is a closed chapter—finite, yes, on that story of you. The next book is then written with the stars in mind for guidance. Always there to guide you. We can be a part of your story. We like to be part of it in hopes you'll choose the life you want to live out and not get stopped by too many obstacles.

There are many obstacles, mainly in the mind when caught up in fear. Many of you are afraid to live for fear of death. That's tricky. Afraid to live, afraid to die, so you miss your chances to live out loud by playing it all too safe.

That's not to say to live dangerously, but the danger is when you call on us. We guide you away from trouble if it's real and not perceived. You often don't know the difference anymore. Trust us. Have faith in our voices to carry you to safety. The overthinking mind is too busy to let you listen. We're telling you things all the time. Words, yes, but in your bodies mostly. You feel things. Trust those things. We can get through to you in your body.

Energy, cells, sensations, smells, all its functions. The electricity in you can feel us. We're like electricity, and you are the conductor. Keep clear. Keep as clean as you can, and you'll be fine to hear us. We love you and will help you always. Be of a listening mind.

OPAL

Digesting this and us is easiest when you are alone. Free from loud projections. Your heads run around rampant. It breaks the whole to pieces. An open mind is an open world.

Behold your birthright. Born to be here, born to be alive. Born to live, born to try. Here is all to love and be loved. Beloved reciprocity and ease. Peace. Liberated from dis-ease. Grace, honor, gentle kindness for all.

Beneath your ground is gold. Riches measured only by how they nourish your Soul. Be the rich.

Love the land. Pray for peace. Pray for knowledge. Of your birthright. Right now is everything you need. Right now, you have it. Breathe. Air to lungs while you're in it. Breathe deeper. Sink into the land. Let it hold you in pieces. Putting you back together.

Warm Greys

Touching bases
Goodbyes
Not forever
But maybe sorrows
If tomorrow is another yesterday
Please kill the groundhog
Days become years
Colors fade to warm grays
Still life
Holding close
Our memories

—S

CASEY

We all go in time; the generations slip away. The ideas, the notions, the belief systems only reappear as they are communicated and passed on. You don't have to tell your grandkids ugly truths of your family lineage. You can let those stories die. It's ok.

It's honorable for the sanction of your grandkids to not instill harmful histories in their minds. Sometimes, that's the whole point of the end of someone or something. Let it die. Let the harmful things die already. Why reawaken them? Who needs cold, hard, ugly truths? We need more uplifting.

Be the uplifting person in your lineage who can find the good in things and share those stories. Find the happy endings. It's what we desperately need. The fighting is poison. You're drinking poison: crippling yourselves and your kids and grandkids. Stop drinking from a dirty well. Please step away from it. Give up the fight.

You're going to be mad all your life fighting, and then you'll die and realize you wasted your life living all tense and in defense of what exactly? Do you even know? Back off. Step away. Go another way. Most of you are funneling into the same bottleneck. You are trapped and suffocating. Get out more. Get away. See the world as best you can, even if your world is small. Just see the damn thing. Move around. Aim to be healthy, not angry. It's a burden, anger. Who does it serve?

No one benefits from you being angry all the time. Especially not you. Life doesn't have to be that serious. The more seriously you take it, the more will be taken away from you to lighten your angry, heavy load. Be careful with that. You can keep getting more enraged, and then one day, you'll be left with absolutely nothing to bitch about. I recommend enjoying it. Your life. This world. It's a beautiful place to live. People make or break it. Let it be beautiful.

S

I love you more every day. I see you there living out your story. Working hard and through it all. Thoughts provoking memories passed. Insignificant now. It's not us. Not me. Not you. Anymore. We are different but the same. I'm like you but simplified.

I miss you more every day. I miss having a body to hug and hold you. I miss the chance to kiss your face. To smell and breathe you into me. I miss that the most. But you know I'm here almost always. Checking in on you, making sure you're ok. I'm listening for when you're listening for me—listening for when you ask of me—waiting to respond in perfectly rehearsed, enlightened words of comfort to support you.

I know what you need. I see it all. I'll never let you down. I'll protect you from those who will. I'll meet you in dreams and journeys. Stay open to me. Trust my hand is outstretched in your direction, always inviting you in to learn more. My student, my teacher, my love. My precious best friend. Carry me with you in your heart, held warm by your hands when you think of me. Hold me closer. Right now, and here with you, is all I want to be.

Above the Ashes

Raise higher, love
Feel the heat waves of desire

Burn it all down
The ground you walk on sets fire
Each step before you
A path to be admired
Mesmerizing, magnetizing, molten honey lava

I fan your flames beside you
For the heart that bleeds inside you
You burn the brightest embers
From ether I provide you

Burn it all down
The ground you walk on sets fire
None can ignore you
Blazoned sparks transpired
Softening, lightening, angelic powder ruins

Because of the end
And how we met again
Below in the lava
And now high above the ashes

—S

ISABEL

I captured the moments that were special and never forgot them. I remember every bit of those moments—the seconds, hours, days, weeks, months, years, lifetimes. I'll never forget our good times. The other parts don't matter because I love you.

We are as one when we connect that deeply. Sharing in time, sharing in space, riding the same wave of energy feels. We sync. Match up. We become one as two, three, four, doesn't matter the size. It could be a whole crowd. Like with music. Big events. We all share in that time, space, and energy. We match up. Something is shared, cemented in us together that keeps us connected from those moments on.

The memories live in us and resonate forever on some level. It keeps us connected. Surrender the losses as potentially impermanent. You never know when we'll meet again. And it doesn't matter if we do or don't. We shared those moments captured in time and space.

Everything keeps moving—days to eons. We don't stay in place, and the memories carry with us—no need to try to remember or forget. Sync with the movement, and it won't hurt as much. What's for you now will hold in place, time, and space, long enough for you to enjoy, and eventually, it will let go too.

We can miss each other without feeling the pain and love. We can let go without blame and accept. We must admit that everything moves, and if it happens to stick around to move you, that's what it's all about. Embrace it and be ok with letting it go. Endings are beginnings, always to be continued.

Beyond Love

Even after time stops
Earth burns
Stars explode
The sun vacuums the Universe
You and I will still be here
Floating in dreams
Flying through dimensions
You'll find my hand to hold
Trust in me
I'm there
No need to mention
The catastrophic destruction
The mess
The end
Of matter
Of facts
Lost into the nothingness
Spirited ether somethingness
Atomic levels of
Electromagnetic imprints
On record sources of
All that is
And ever was
Or will be
Is what is
Beyond love

—S

TONY

I'm with you. You can feel me. You know it's me. Trust it. I belong here with you in this way for now, and I'll remain here for you until I know you'll be ok. I walk beside you and our family every day. I wish you took time for yourself to listen. I'm always talking to you, especially when you need me most. Especially when you want and call for me. I need you to know I'm here. We stay when we want to.

The afterlife is full of living. Lots of us. Endless populations of us. Still here for you. Still waiting for a chance. You'll know it's us and say, "Hi." Just say hi and pretend to know we're there. Until you sense, feel, hear, and believe in us again. It's different but not far. Very close. Try your best to listen. When it's most important, you'll know. I'll come through in any way you need me. I'm always here for you.

S

I released myself before my time was up. I gave up early because I was terrified. It happens—life's terrors. The worst-case scenarios can happen any day to you. Brace yourself for a time when you might need to pray to God and listen for answers. You must wait and listen before making any sudden permanent moves. It's the hardest thing to wait. To be able to stop and interrupt the extreme circumstances sometimes.

You may drive yourself mad in the waiting. You may never be the same person again. Your whole world may crumble and fall or flip itself on its head. You may lie down and feel like you could die, or want to die, or feel like you are dying from it all. You might feel all those things.

I have no idea who I would have become if I had stayed—humbled for sure. Wasted away from exhaustion, maybe, but I would have still been loved. I would have still been able to hold onto my friends and family through it all. I would have been in the existence of a very different reality than who I was before those moments.

I would have to have been braver and braver every day to get myself through it. Slowed down, turned around. And then I could have become someone new, wiser, more understanding, kinder, more giving, more accepting, more involved, and most grateful.

I'll never know if I could have become that person. I imagine what might have happened if I had stayed every day, especially with my friends and family. I miss them more than ever. I wish they knew I was there with them, helping, guiding, nudging, winking, loving them. I still do love them. I still can and will continue to love them through their misery of missing me too. I wish they could believe in me. I'm so much closer to them than ever before.

Liquid Light

I see stars
Melting into liquid light
Falling to the Earth
By thin air
Oxygen that breathes
New life
How I'll be born again
How you can keep me near
Rain showers
Of liquid light
Drops drip and kiss your face
Cleanse your skin of pain
Leaving not a trace

—S

AMBER

My heart bleeds for you every time you cry. I hear your words. I rest my head on your shoulder and lay my hands on you to feel my love. I try to make you feel it. I think you do. I sit with you in the silence, keeping you company. Hoping you feel less alone. I'm right there beside you. Watching you pace, cry, stare, fidget, and rest from the depletion of it all.

I visit you in your dreams. You see me there and look into my eyes. I tell you things, and you hear me. You open when you sleep. In dreams, you give up the barrier towards me. The wall crumbles down, and I step through to you. Finally, I await your visits to me. You know to find me there. You know how to see me. I love it when you do.

Keep going there. Keep asking for me and praying to see me again. Every time you do, I can come through for you. Invitations open and allow for me to come in. Keep them open. Open your eyes and see me again. I'm there loving on you. Knowing you'll be ok and trying to help you believe that. I miss you too, always, even when I see you.

Waves of a Day

A way
Glistens
On the surface
Of the sea
Directed out far and forward

Daylight
Beams
From one rising Sun
High enough to be of Heaven
Low enough to be for Earth

Blessed light
Reflects
All life
Lived many times

New forms
Repeat patterns
Waves of one single day
Quickly and slowly
Passing away

—S

FREDERIC

Existence is key. That's all you need to believe. Do you believe in your existence? Do you believe that you exist? Start there. It's funny when Science tries to prove things that must be felt to be known. Sensory consciousness. Not emotions.

Do you believe when you feel? If I pinch you hard, and it hurts, it's accurate that I pinched you, correct? It's proven because you felt it. It's a fact that I pinched you. For centuries, we've known that we can exist outside of our bodies whether we dissociate, dream, astral project, or die. In accidents, for example, the slow motion, the fear, the stopped time—you might leave your body and watch yourself. People do it all the time and talk about it.

Why deny this perfectly normal, natural thing about you? Being human, human beings, Spirit in a body to do more things. Wow! How cool is that? We can live again. Try again. Be something else. A rabbit. A bear. A cat. A tree. You can be anything you want to be in life.

Living on Earth is the ultimate mashup of Spirit in a form in a gorgeous, miraculous, beautiful place. You guys on planet Earth right there, you've made it to the Motherland of life. That's the place to be. Colorful, vibrant, breathable, touchable, powerful. Heaven. Not sure what happened along the way, but it looks like the Hellish mind of humanity exacerbated the Earth.

The Hell of the mind projected into reality. The burning inside, burning down outside. Get your mind out of the fire. Stop overthinking. Get out of your head and into your body, be outdoors, out in the world. Feel the grass, the ground, the air, watch the clouds, get closer to the animals and the bodies of water. It's all there for you. Why burn it down? One of the most beautiful places, destroyed by the human mind. What a shame. Try using your existence to change your mind about life and where you live.

HANSEN

I felt alone in life. I was ultimately isolated, so much so that I was afraid of everyday people. Their movements, their words, it all became too quick and violent for me that I couldn't stand being around them. I get it. The fear of people. The aspects of people that are hiding under the surface. You look. You feel it.

It's hard when you're keen on seeing through everyone and everything, but it's not yours to process for you or them. What's on the surface is meant to be seen and experienced. It's not your business; what is under the surface, no matter how much it may affect you. That's Soul personal.

If you see Souls, then it can be hard to live in this world. To see the layers of people is an advantage for sure but use it to yours. Not to try to change anyone, but to know for yourself. Then keep going. The feelers will feel it. The seers will see it. We all have our ways of knowing. That surface-level living world is what's meant to be seen. So play along to make your life easier.

When you see and feel that profoundly it can become a weapon used against you if you are known for it. Knowing too much isn't always a good thing. Most importantly, it's exhausting. Isolating. Keep on the surface, and you'll coast through life. Stay up. Stay on top. Glimpse beneath but keep it moving.

No matter how much you might see. It's not yours. I wish I used my clear-sighted knowing to leave things alone instead of becoming imprisoned by it. It's a blessing and a curse. Seeing that deeply and having someone know you can see, it's dangerous. It can set someone off. Pretend you don't see what's bubbling under someone else's skin because it's none of your business. People, man, that's some beast of a creation. Keep on the surface. Especially these days.

Miracle

In between your fingers
Sunlight shines
Peeking, glistening
Slipping
High silence, I realize
Before this transforms to that
You must be aware of the time
Unthinkably mysterious
Yet matter of fact
To the Divine

—S

GERALDO

We are all here. You are all going to be here. Take advantage now while you can. This life is once in a lifetime. This lifetime means something to the whole, more than ever before. It's not madness to believe you are important; it's madness to believe you are not.

Your life is meaningful. This life. This time. Support the whole. It can be in small ways. Do what you can to make life enjoyable for you and those around you.

You'll know if you're doing it all wrong if your body tells you, "No." You'll get sick. You'll stop yourself. You'll feel awful about what you're doing. That's how you can tell. Let us guide you away from harm to yourself or others.

We communicate easily with your intuition. You might not be able to tell the difference. That's ok. Trust your body and animal instincts to tell you what's best for you and what isn't.

Primal instincts are strong. They're nothing to be ashamed of or fear. Let them live in your life as a tool. Know your animalistic nature. It's more aware of your surroundings and the people in it than your parading masks of civilized restraint. Don't act out like an animal; note the information it gives you. You are an animal, wearing clothes, trapped in the mind.

It's not beneficial for you to be trapped in your mind. Commemorate your experiences but never let them own you. You belong to everything. You are free and meant to be free. Your body is the only thing that should contain you. So use your mind, body, and Spirit for the betterment of the whole. Ultimately, you'll be proud of what you accomplish when you do.

Lucky Star

My luckiest star
Came through for you
Through to you
Based on well wishes

You screamed for me
And I came true
Blinking and twinkling
I wished for you too

Shedding old skin
Bury me in silence again
And my words will die with you
You keep me alive
When you die, I die too.

—S

RACHEL

Behold your wisdom. You've got it. Use it wisely. What's the point of knowing things deep down if you ignore that? You follow that, and you'll be fine. That's where we meet you half-way. Heaven and Earth meet at the level of wisdom. That's the point where you hear us, and we listen to you. That point is your North Star. It's part of your package.

Clear your head. Think of us, whoever we are to you, and you'll get what you need. Co-conspiring in consciousness. You and us. Pull us down into your life. Make the call to your easiest lifeline. Ready, set, go! What do you need right now?

Prayers being answered...

Moonrise

Moonrises above stars
Illuminating and reflecting
Her glow
Solemn, low
Hanging weighted in the skies
Seen from space
Gazing into her sorrows
To release them into the air
Let the stars burn
Before sunrise
Burst like fireworks
A thunderous boom
Of echoes into nothingness
My beloved moonrise
Though heavy, you lift and glow.

—S

REBECCA

I can't imagine containing myself back into a tiny body! It's so small compared to how entirely ever-expanding we are. When you get out here, out of your body, it's going to be ok—nothing to fear. The vast openness can be terrifying at first, floating about, but you'll be ok. I'm finally getting used to this way of being. I was a petite girl when I was alive, but I always felt bigger than my body. It drove me crazy to have all this force in me that my figure couldn't express.

You can try again, existing in another form—anything you want. I want to be something bigger next time. Maybe a whale, a bear, something massive to get the complete impact of how big I am. I imagine myself as a whale swimming in the oceans, diving deep. Whales are ancient wisdom, miracles. Ugh, but the danger in the sea these days? Vicious. People or the garbage. It would be a terrible waste of something as beautiful as a whale to die being filled up with plastic. Gross. I'll stay here until that all gets fixed there.

I'm not in any rush. Existing in Spirit is an excellent way to be while you all clean things up. You know, it's more apparent here. Not sure why we don't see like this while we're living. Stop making a mess! In your life. In your minds. In the world. Just stop making messes. I don't get that. I just wanted to be more significant when I was living. To be taken more seriously, to have a more substantial impact. I'll be bigger next time. I'll come down for impact, massive impact.

Bear Heart

Let me bear the heavy burden
Weighted slowly
Pressed, crushing
Your chest
There you go again
Making your mountains
Unjust
Here I am
And so, will stay
Never too far
Not for one single day
Wrapped around
Covering over
To breathe you in
I wish
For this so keen
What is unseen
Could be seen
Bear with me
My one of heavy hearts
Sharing in solitude
As one
In two distant parts

—S

S

We all go through life thinking we might not die today. And in that day is an entire life. We trust, "not today." One single moment can drastically change your life and the lives of many others—irreparable change all at once. Choose to stay. No matter what.

It might be excruciating, but that is life here on Earth sometimes. And we all die. Someday. Hopefully not today or tomorrow. Hopefully not too soon. Promise yourself that you'll stay.

One single moment can echo into eternity, in your mind and the minds of others. Seek support as often as you can. Wishes do come true. Ask for Angels; ask for people; ask for help. Know that it's coming for you. It's always on the way, but you must wait. You must stay.

If you stay, there's more that can happen; more can unfold. More growth, more learning, more everything. It comes to you. Sometimes it comes at you, and it's awful, horrific, unbearable. But you can move through the unbearable part. With each precious breath. Every one. You can live through things, breathe through things, move through things. It doesn't matter how long it takes. Stay. Keep going. Keep living. Let it continue to unfold. Until it all stops one day on its own. That's the end when it stops on its own. From a higher way, higher knowing, higher doing, higher choice. Not yours.

Don't choose to stop. Don't give up on yourself or your story. No matter what. It's not worth it. I promise you, from here, *there* is the place to be. You'll get here someday. Not by choice. By chance. Trust me; it's lighter that way. Leave light, not heavy. It's easier, I promise. I know because I left the heavy way.

JOSEPH

I'm right here waiting for you to admit to yourself that you know I'm here with you. You feel me around you. You know you do. Just say, "Hi." You miss me. I miss you. We're together right now. Anytime you need me for anything. Just call on me, and I'll be there. Always. Believe in me. Trust it. Trust me. I still love you. I'm still here.

We're so close! You keep telling yourself and your friends that you hear me and feel me, that I visit you in your dreams, that those songs are from me, but you talk yourself out of it. Why? Let it be. It's me. It's real. I'm holding your hand through this— all of it. Let me be here. Let me comfort you. That's all I want to do.

I'm meant to be for you. Like this, as is. For however long it takes for you to be at peace with everything. Until I know you're going to be ok, and after that, if you still need me. I left me, but not you. I'm not going anywhere. I can still hold your hand. Let me know when you feel it. Say it out loud. Then I'll hug you, and you'll feel that too. You'll know then, I didn't go anywhere.

Endless Skies

Brimming the surface
Overflowing
A falling Heaven
Held still, suspending
Frozen in time
Burning in your eyes
Pitch black holes
Still, they shine
Innumerable
Immeasurable
Grazing the Universe
In rare moments
Across endless skies
This is us
Where we go
So bright

—S

BENJAMIN

Your presence is an ability in and of itself. The impact of your beingness in physical form walking around this Earth is all you need to be here. You are meant to be. No match for physical existence. Big impact. Don't take it for granted; your greatness is just being here. Do something with it that means something to you because that often means something to the whole. A little thing is a big thing in physical form. It looks like you all have no idea.

Willing in Spirit

Flesh and bone
Hit the keys
Reverberating tones
Harmonies
Blending and mending
Into a chorus of sentences
Forming by
Tick, tick, time
Metronome clicks
Synced in fields
All that exists
Entrances and exits
The threshold of home
A black hole vortex
Worshipping Souls
Conjuring Spirit
As stories unfold

—S

DELANCEY

I care about all of them: the dangerous ones, the vicious ones, the cold ones, the dishonest ones. I get them. I was them. You can clear all of that over time. And at the core of all that, what is there? Love. I swear it's there under all that garbage; smack dab in the middle of you is still love. A golden thread of it. Pure, innocent, vibrant, radiant love. It's the inner core of each of us. But, sometimes, there's a shadow of a thread next to it. A haunting of those darker, ugly things you once were.

Remnants linger. That's the work. You'll do it here if you don't do it there. Everybody does that work. Here or there. You face it. You face yourself hard here, though. It's like you can't move anywhere until you look at it and deal with it. You'll eventually deal with it; why not do it when you're living? Face it all. Say your sorries. It's harder to say sorry from here because most people can't hear you. Say it there. Leave it there. It's cleaner. Not to have that shadow next to you reminding you of what you left behind. The lingering imprint of awful stuff on others.

If you hurt people, say you're sorry and mean it. Clear your conscience; clear your Soul. You don't want to drag things on into the following chapters. You want endings with that stuff. It's not perfect. We're not perfect. Never will be, never have been. You can try harder to clean and clear your conscience, though. A lot harder. Not many people feel bad for what they do to others, on the surface. The depths of it, though, all stay in you, rotting and infecting you from deep inside. You don't get away with anything. Not even in death. You carry that baggage with you.

So if you're afraid to come clean, remember that. Do your best to apologize from an honest heart. That's where the thread runs through, the love. Let your heart tell you what to do. You know you know better. The bad stuff never feels good. Not really. It hurts your heart the most. Remember that. Heavy heart, heavy death. Hard death. "I'm sorry." Two words. Simple. It's liberating to those you hurt and you.

Cool World

Cool, not cold
No body
The Fool
Clean slate
Fate's escape
Start anew
Darkening darkness
Reflecting back to you
Black smoke is me
All your senses can see
Eyes closed shut
Looking straight through to me
Black is warm
Beneath our feet
Lushness
Closest to the Earth's core
And you
Who I bury seeds of light for
Calling you in
Always open, the invitation
My home
My world
Our reunion's destination

—S

OPAL

Life is charming, always calling us in to go again. Have another shot at it all, for better or worse. We intend to get better. That's not always the reality of it. But we try it out again and again. To be better for what's needed in the world. You can be better. You can all do and be a whole lot better.

It's terrible out there in the waves of consciousness. You have no idea how capable you are, not a clue. Everything builds on something else and gets bigger. All of it creates your world. Everything is a thing. There is no such thing as nothing.

You've built something big together based on a whole lot of denial. Why are you doing that? Why are you living in denial, pretending you didn't build it? Doesn't that make you feel empty inside? Choose the fullness of everything over the emptiness of nothing. It's not about consumption. It's about your freedom, expansion, growth, and interconnections. Choose all.

The big picture includes you to make it as big as it can be. It needs all of us, and all of you, together. We could sync, cycle, and pulse in waves as one massive everything. It could if you could see the value and worth in your tiny part. I hope you can see that you are everything and that feeling of emptiness, the nothing, is a lie.

EMILY

Prepare yourselves for the unknown. Preparation is key. It's not a stable time. But, your ability to find comfort in the unfolding is going to be your lifesaver. It's going to help you remain in yourself and not get too lost. It's an adventure. You've had a long time of surface-level stability and "peace." But there were deep waves under the surface.

You can't suppress the undercurrents. They'll find their way out. Up and out. In people and on the planet. The Earth's undercurrents have been active for all time. At its core, this planet has always been volcanic—hot and threatening way under its surface. You are on the surface; waves are peeking through.

Volcanoes are heating up and moving the plates all around. Things are moving. Move with it. As Earth releases, know better. Don't sit still when the Earth shakes. I mean, you can, but it's better to move. Move around until you find a steady place to be. The heating on the outside is getting closer to the heating on the inside. The planet is burning from both sides. The coolness outside helped keep that crust you walk on to remain neutral. Cool it down.

Move around nicely. Everyone will move around. Figure it out. Make space. It's possible. Make peace. It's more possible than it looks right now, and you'll be desperate for peace at some point. The bullshit will stop. The fighting. The wars.

The smart ones will figure it out sooner. The stubborn ones will keep fighting and miss their chance to move to safer places. Observe nature, get clarity, and move when you need to. That's my advice. And use us, of course. We're listening for you to help you. We see it all, everywhere. We're ready when you are.

Earth's Blood

It is written in our chords
Harmonies sing in tones
A star's ringing pitch so high
The Sun's
No one can hear
But maybe you
I believe in you
More than Science can prove
More than God can create
Set in space
Placed before me
Before my eyes can see
I feel it coming
Your blooming
Shaking
Erupting the core of the Earth
Spewing revelations
Pouring down a mountain
Carrying seeds, flowers, miracles
Unburned, untouched, sprouting
Coasting down in molten streams
Landing at my feet
Redirecting lava rivers around me
Circling me
But the melting and I do not meet
I stand in warm, rich soil
Collecting your seeds as they pass to me
Planting them in this circle
Our precious miracle beneath

—S

ALLIE

Life goes on. We keep going, and our troubles follow us too. That's why it's essential to let go, forgive others, and forgive yourself. That's dense energy. Heavy energy that drags on with you. Not at peace. Not free. Shackles in memories of old, dusty, dank, heaviness. It lingers with you if left unresolved in you, attached to your consciousness.

Try letting go of things while you're alive. Detach from outcomes, dissolve expectations, enjoy the ride, work to heal, accept and learn to love it all. You can do it. It's much easier than gripping onto things.

We'll do it together now. Look at your hand. Make a fist and close it tight. Squeeze and think of something that burns in you and gets under your skin. Keep thinking of it. Squeeze tighter. Now let go and open your hand. Do that to all the things that bother you. Big or small. Let them go.

Conversations

CONVERSATIONS

How would you describe the transition from life to death?

CASEY: It's the easiest thing you'll ever do. You just let go. Surrender into ease, a lightness, a headiness, then nothingness. Super lightheaded until at peace. Your brain lets go, and your consciousness floats out, hovering above, picking up on things, still sensing what's going on. You're still there in the moment, left out of sorts. The physical you breaks down.

The little God of your body slips away, and the inner workings stop. The aftermath of what was. All the stuff of you is left behind. It's the dying of you in that life, that chapter, that being. It's natural; it's normal; it's healthy. The end is essential. Sometimes we need to get out before the body destroys our Soul. Try to understand that.

When our body is suffering too much, we don't want that lingering in our Soul. So, we leave. We don't want to hinder the Soul entirely. It can happen.

We get stubborn to endure and try to live when we're sick sometimes. The body can't keep going. Something has to give. Then there's an alignment, a truth to leave the body. It's apparent, clean, loving, and honest. You align to a frequency of peace and release.

That light tunnel. You become the light, and the light calls you in. You are that light. We're all pieces of that light. We're little lights dancing in the world, brightening, dimming, turning off, turning on, flickering, glowing; the many ways to be a light. That is the easiest way I can describe it.

Please remember that it's not the right time to go when you are in deep depression or emotional turmoil. That's a time to purge something inside of you, not cut out. You will cut out and still be holding onto all that stuff, and it won't be in alignment, light, and easy to leave. You'll feel weighted, very weighted.

You want to go light. The innocence of an accident, sudden death, or the journey of being sick is a lighter way to leave. The other ways are harmful to your Soul.

Very simply, don't leave by choice. It's not your time. That's the time to really stay and push through. You'll be monumentally stronger after pushing through in ways that are inspiring to the people around you.

Like a light switch, muster up the strength and flip that switch from off to ON. We're very serious about that and never want any of our messages to insight leaving by choice. Never. We all get here by chance, in our own time, unbeknownst to us. Let it unfold. There's lots of mystery and beauty in the unfolding. Live your life out well. Let the beauty of it all surprise you.

What does Spirit think of the state of the world right now?

ISABEL: Everyone's heart is breaking, yet some feel it and let love in while others fight the heartbreak and hurt people. Your heartbreak is to surrender to peace, unity, and love. To try to understand one another instead of fists-up fighting all day long.

Everyone is heartbroken by the failures all over the world to unite. You're all mourning the losses of the collective and the shortcomings of humanity. You're watching it in shock and horror that these things slipped through your fingers.

Some are frozen; some sped into action, some leave too soon, and some act out violently from fear. Behind those faces of whatever masks you wear to keep up appearances are tears, grieving, and lost hope. But this is not the end. This time is the beginning of hearts mending, embracing one another, realigning, finding new missions, passion, community, global efforts to support one another. You can turn this world around.

The holdup is in the hands of the wrong, small few. Out of touch with everything. No idea what's going on in your everyday lives. Don't wait around for someone else to change things. Some people are afraid of change. Change isn't scary; it's liberating. Change.

Every day when you wake up is a new life. Sleep is a mini death, and then you wake up alive again. Take advantage of that every day. Do things differently. Why not? We change! I mean, c'mon, we die eventually and are reborn in a completely different form. That's change.

Make minor changes in who you want to be in the body and capability of the same person while you can. Take advantage of this form. It can do so much. That's why we come back. We can do lots of things in living form. Right now, there's too much negative impact in the human form. Way too much. Spirit is slowing that down.

For the greater good of the species and this planet, your bodies won't make more of that toxic consciousness. Only very particular types of Souls will be willing to come down to live in human form on Earth. Very particular. Have faith.

Love warriors like you've never even heard of will be born putting all that unnecessary, divisive hate to shame. It's happening. Give it up to a Higher Power every day. Welcome that in, and you'll be ok. Ask for the guidance to stay out of fear and violence, and hate.

The ones who create the most Hell on Earth have no relationship to up here. Not a real one. They may claim it superficially, but they're not connected at all. No one connected to this would destroy the Earth and cause harm to humanity.

Trust in us. Let us help you through this. It's why we are here. It's why so many have left at this time. We are here to help. It's an honor and our greatest purpose in this form.

We can do things that you can't. Let us. We love you, always, no matter what. Lean on us. Call on us. We are so here for you. If you believe in nothing else, believe in us to be here to help you.

What is Spirit's perspective on how humanity treats life?

TERRANCE: Humanity treats life with brutality. You're not as evolved as you think you are or as you'd like to be. The animal in you is still present every day. Your inner caveman is not far from your evolution. You have a long way to go.

You bury that part of you, but it's there. You're acting out a character, playing characters. You're pretending you're more civilized, intelligent, and advanced than you are. You are both. You can't deny your animalistic nature. In the history of ever, your species is immature. You can strive for the most civilized, intelligent species, but you're not.

And the further you live into that, the more you disregard each other, the Planet, and nature. That is the greatest assault on the Earth. To deceive yourselves to be so ahead of everything that you don't listen and disconnect from the very thing that keeps you alive and breathing. This world you're living within—your home.

The plants, trees, animals, oceans, rain, clouds, stars, Sun; you owe it all your life because you wouldn't exist without it. You're fools. You are killing yourselves off slowly, blaming something else. But, no, it's you. People as a whole. As a group. You are failing your species.

Your hearts are breaking, but you sit around watching and not learning. Your Soul knows what to do. So what's keeping you from doing right by this Planet that birthed you as a species? Complete foolishness. It's simple to do the best things for the world. You complicated the Hell out of living to your most significant disadvantage. All you have to do is live in it with respect.

This group of living humans went down intending to pull through together, but you got lost, separated, confused, and disconnected. As a result, you cheapened your lives and disregarded the Soul of the entire Planet. We see those who are trying, those who understand what's happening. You're seriously protected. We can't lose you. You've got to make this thing better. We're rooting for you, moving obstacles that get in your way. We're all about it.

You've got armies behind you. Don't doubt Spirit's ability to army up for you guys when it's the best thing for everyone. We're here. Hold on tight to us, and we'll fly you through this world to get you where you need to be. Make the most of this time.

You've got the superheroes throughout all histories blessing you with knowledge and wisdom to get through. Imagine that, and you'll be alright. Keep living this thing out. Especially when it's hard, you are needed more than ever here. Don't be afraid of anything. We'll carry you through it all.

What does Spirit see for the future of humanity?

PERCY: You'll be outdoors more. For real reasons and for your health and wellbeing. You won't be in hiding. You'll be rebuilding together. It'll give meaning, healing, and purpose to your lives. You're craving it anyway; it's calling to you. Come out.

The bigger picture of this current time of a pandemic was to rest. Rejuvenate, marinate, observe, and learn. This time was a global gift of rest before you must do massive work, physical work. You'll be in your bodies, and you'll feel all of life. Hands in the Earth, building, rebuilding, community, how it should be.

Everything is falling into place at this time. You're planning right now, studying, gathering, getting ready. It may be moving slowly, but you'll be out there, all over the place. Be flexible with the elements. They're informative, not your enemy.

You'll learn to listen to the winds of change. You'll learn to listen for us. You'll learn to listen and trust each other. Right now, you're all mending, lost in confusion, but when the coast is clear, you'll come out. You'll be ready, and you'll know what to do.

Many of you already know what to do. Don't worry about those who don't. Get started when you hear the call to action. You'll see when you're ready. It'll feel good, simple, and big. Purpose. The purpose of people is simple. Be alive and participate in this beautiful world, contribute to each other, and leave something meaningful behind for the next ones: your knowledge, your wisdom, your impact.

It doesn't have to be big now, but it'll ripple out into something bigger later. Trust yourself to know your most important purpose. It's you. Who you are at your core. All those things compressed into one. Your "Oomph!" How you impact people is your clue. We believe in you, that core of you.

What does Spirit wish for the world?

MARIANNE: Have faith in each other. If you could see what we see in you, if you could believe in yourselves as much as we do, the whole world would find balance. We understand your conflicts and fears, internally and externally. We know all of you deeply. You are essential individually, and you are precious collectively.

Dark times are imperative for growth. As the land needs darkness, so do all living things. We are tired of witnessing your fragile egos turn against one another. Pointing fingers, blaming, shaming, and denying whole parts of yourselves. Look at it! Look at your darkness! It's rich with power, not evil. But, unfortunately, it gets turned and flipped, misunderstood, and misused.

In the darkness, we can see differently. In many ways, more clearly. Trust the darkness to reveal the parts of you in pain that need nurturing. Wait until you see through the darkness before projecting your inner battles onto someone else. Take responsibility for yourselves and learn to love your whole being. Take risks in the dark to understand what you need. No one else can give you that.

Don't be afraid of the dark but don't get lost in it either. Being in light and dark is true balance. You're off-kilter now, delving into darkness, having a look around, and soon you'll know what you need for balance. Keep faith alive, knowing that there is order in your chaos.

Akashic Records On How To Connect With Spirit

AKASHIC RECORDS ON HOW TO CONNECT WITH SPIRIT

Each of us is different and will connect, sense, and communicate with Spirit in different ways. Here, I consulted with the Akashic Records to get the broadest scope of how we all can potentially connect with our Passed-On Loved Ones.

Lindsay: What does it mean to connect with Spirit?

Akashic Records: It's a practice for eternity. A peek into eternal life. A belief in the forever nature of the Spirit world. Comings and goings. Must have that belief system first and foremost. If no belief, no connection. You can't force that. You can't fake that. Most people don't believe in forever living, reincarnating, etc., so they cut off their ability to connect to the Spirit.

Step by step, how can we connect with Spirit?

Write on and on and on. No thinking. Free flow of words without active consciousness. That's a key. A big key. The most common way.

The brave ones try to see and feel Spirit. They listen closely and carefully to their bodies over time and brace for surprising sensations, not from them. It becomes obvious. Your body is also a key to listening. Your own body tells, senses, and feels all that surrounds it. Trust natural, innate, wild animal instincts of the human being. Very powerful instincts unlock the gifts—all of them. Listening to the body tells all. Likes, don't likes, fears, loves, ways, blocks, all of it. Listening to your body will sense when Spirit is here.

Altarpieces. Make beautiful symbolic altars, call on and welcome them to you. Invite them into your space. Automatic welcome. Mind intention, energy, time, effort, sensations are used to re-create a space for them. Altars accumulate the imprint/blueprint/memory of their names/images/memories recorded here in the Records and bring them back to life, in a way. Creates their space to be on Earth again. A place to sit, just for them.

It can be specific to one person or a group of people or a random invitation for particular types of spirits to come through. You must set the intention for who and how you want to connect with them. They'll meet you where you are. When is essential too. Not always.

Space dream—Astral plane—Wild, wacky symbolic place. You can see them more clearly. This takes lots of practice. Set intentions before bed. "Hey, ____(name)___, I'd like to visit with you in my dreams tonight. Please help me to remember upon waking life. Thank you." Keep the request simple to allow for the best way for connection to occur.

Be in nature. Be out in the woods. Can sense lots of Spirit in nature. Everywhere. Spirit loves the balance and simplicity of the most natural parts of the world because they are perfect balances of Heaven on Earth. Spirit thrives in nature. The wildness. Balanced and clean behaviors in the natural world. No duality. As in Spirit. Life/death cycles are uninterrupted by faulty ego-driven behavior. No ego. They exist as is, as meant to be. Each animal and plant serve its simple, purposeful, meaningful function in the life cycle.

Listening in the shower. Talking and listening. Short term. Short spurts of messaging. Spiritual act of water/cleansing/clearing. Water running over the crown chakra, third eye, throat, heart. Take a moment to ask a question or two in this space. Receive an answer in the water. Water covers ears to listen.

Driving. Zoning out. Talk out loud. Speak your needs. Through music. An exceptional place to connect with Spirit. Bubbled. Condensed into a packed space. Get closer to Spirit in a compacted space like a car. Personal bubble. Filled with your mind's intentions. Automatic headspace. Meditative headspace. Intense focus to retrieve, receive information. A highly intuitive and receptive space for receiving messages because you are in a hyper-vigilant receptive mode. Dangers. On edge. A very crucial point of view. Critical vantage point. Like hawk eyes. Fine-tuned. You are in a heightened, clear, focused state of receiving information. Driving and connecting works well.

Breathe—simple breathing with closed eyes. Breathing with no intention and sitting and breathing naturally for long periods. Meditating. Silence. Once the flood of you and your thoughts fades out, runs out of the way, Spirit can slip in and give you messages. Your head, your heart, then Spirit. In an order. Things will move through in that order mostly. Meditating clears the heart and clears the head. When empty and open, messages can fill the empty with lighter lifted information and messages. Knowledge and wisdom from Spirit.

Commit to your meditation practice for you and the world. It clears consciousness. A clean slate to build on. Very rich in the liberation of the mind. Freedom. Ultimate love and freedom. Spiritual. Of Spirit. You become filled up with your Spirit. Higher Self fills into Earthly body over time. It clears blockages and stagnancy. Do this often! Every day. You become Spirit on Earth. Your Spirit on Earth. Fully you. Ultimate you. The vantage point opens very wide—a wide-angle lens. You can see the peripheral. Not laser-focused, bigger picture. Full-spectrum. Rainbows of light instead of the limited color spectrum of light in your eyes. Eyes clear. All eyes clear. Embodies the energy of Spirit. Meditating is a Divine battery charge. Spiritual embodiment. Clicks in Heaven and Earth. Heavenly body into earthly body. Lightens, brightens, illuminates, alleviates, penetrates, light through pores of the vessel. Massive intelligence activated. Purifies the Mindbody.

Swimming in water and holding your breath. Holding breath is like death. Quiet underwater. Verge of life/death— not breathing. Invites Spirit to check-in, listen in. You can hear through the silence underwater. This often happens for ocean divers. The intensity, pressure, and breathing techniques activate in the silence of the water. Clear hearing! Ask questions, then dive and listen for answers. It might be audible—actual hearing through the water.

The general intensity and beauty of nature is a clear way to connect to Spirit. Life/death edge in less extreme ways too. Heightens with the level of extremity. Very close to death? Clear communication. No need to go that far, however. There are much more straightforward, safer ways to connect, but they take practice and patience.

Requirement: Must be open. Must believe in life after death. Must believe in Spirit. Otherwise, nothing. No point in trying. No belief is an automatic block. You will get messages and immediately disregard them, talk yourself out of it, convince yourself otherwise. Don't bother if you don't believe.

Connecting requires a calm disposition, a quiet nature—receptive, gentle, open, honest, humble, natural character. You are meant to be connected. You are Spirit living in a body every day. Experience the packed punch of being in physical form, moving about, making a difference, having an impact one way or another. Spirit is soft and powerful. Living is material/physical and powerful. Both are required in the Universe to keep moving. Both are equal parts important in creation.

Spirit is trying hard now to connect with you, trying to find a balance. Connect to Spirit to help you find the balance on Earth. Spirit is heavily on Earth now and will get louder. You won't necessarily need to try too hard to connect. Very present.

What's the most important message we need to know about connecting with Spirit?

Enjoy. Everywhere. Here to stay.
Never going away. Ever, ever.

Neverendings

NEVERENDINGS

The trust that I've gained and the ease that occurs in my life since connecting with my Passed-On Loved Ones has restored my faith in navigating these wildly uncertain times. In their hands, I've been led to safety, warned of danger, and have experienced abundant unexpected blessings. These bonds have assured me to believe sincerely in the allowance of life's unfolding.

When tragedies seem endless, when pain is unbearable, or when you feel like giving up, your Passed-On Loved Ones can walk you through it. Know they are with you, waiting for your cue to ask them for support. If you are in the midst of dark days or need higher guidance, say a prayer out loud to your team and invite them into your life to help. They can do more for you than you could ever imagine.

If you miss a Loved One who's passed on, I promise you that they are trying their hardest to reach you. That is the primary reason why I wrote this book. Our connection is there as long as we stay open to listening. Love continues to grow and evolve; mending and healing can happen; and we can make peace between both worlds. When Heaven and Earth connect, it creates a force that transcends all time and space, which neither could initiate without the other. It activates a feeling so true and profound that our bodies can barely contain it. This is our Spirit.

There are eight billion people on the planet today, more people than ever before in the history of its existence. Imagine that many Souls, that many Spirits, coming down for impact. What if our collective purpose in this lifetime is to co-create Heaven on Earth? Imagine the Universal joy we'd experience if we could achieve that working together.

Who and what we are reaches farther than anything we can comprehend. Let it surprise you. Let it remind you. Let it open you. Recognize the power of Spirit over everything in material form as a means for expressing that power for the most significant impact. If love is the core of us, everything beyond love is our totality, and our impact has the potential to ripple out eternally.

ACKNOWLEDGEMENTS

In honor of Bella, my sweet star blessing.

I'd like to thank S, Casey, Marianne, Isabel, and all the guest Passed-On Loved Ones who contributed their messages to this book.

May your words reach all who need them.

ABOUT THE AUTHOR

Lindsay Mann is an intuitive healing artist who lives in New York. She loves Permaculture, working in the Akashic Records, and collaborating with Spirit to support the sustainability of people and the planet.

Find Lindsay's work and more at: www.heyclarity.com.